LOVE NOTES
for the REJECTED
to rescue your heart and renew your hope

Copyright © 2015 Angie Wynn. All rights reserved. No portion of this book may be reproduced mechanically, electronically, or by any other means, including photocopying, without written permission of the publisher. It is illegal to copy this book, post it to a website, or distribute it by any other means without permission from the publisher.

Angie Wynn
authorangiewynn@gmail.com
www.angiewynn.com

Remember to join my mailing and be one of the first 500 readers to get your FREE download of *"Out of Darkness"* by Cindy Grate.

Limits of Liability and Disclaimer of Warranty

The author and publisher shall not be liable for your misuse of this material. This book is strictly for informational and educational purposes. The author and/or publisher do not guarantee that anyone following these techniques, suggestions, tips, ideas, or strategies will become successful. The author and/or publisher shall have neither liability nor responsibility to anyone with respect to any loss or damage caused, or alleged to be caused, directly or indirectly by the information contained in this book.

Cover Design – Marlon Trone

Printed in the United States

ISBN 978-1-941749-44-9

4-P Publishing

Chattanooga, TN 37411

Endorsements

What can I say about Angie Wynn? This is a woman of grace and peace who speaks the truth with unfailing integrity. She has a heart for the least and the lost as well as for those who have stuff and no serenity. Angie is 'right on' as a counselor and has given her life to encouraging and guiding those who will listen. May her tribe increase. We need more Angie Wynns!

Jan Silvious-Author of "Same Life New Story"

Acknowledgments

To My Loving Heavenly Father- Where would I be without You? I continue to be overwhelmed by Your Mercy, Your Grace and Your Love. Thank You for everything!

My Mom, Linda Reeves - Thank you for being the willing vessel to get me here. I know it wasn't easy. I love you and I am grateful.

My Brother, Marlon Trone - You are the best brother ever. I love you and Sydney with my whole heart.

Thomasina Coley – You changed my life for eternity. I love you for leading me out of darkness into His love.

Ken Edwards - Thank you for your Counsel, your patience, your friendship. So many times you resuscitated me. You loved me to life!

Jan Silvious - Your encouragement always blesses me. I have never been invisible to you.

My publishing coach, Laura Bester Brown -You're the best! Thank you for your expertise!

Mandy Coley, Kelley Morgan-Hayton, and Carolyn Capp - It was so much more than Editing! Thank you for affirming the language of my heart.

To My Pastors, Teachers, Mentors and Friends - You have prayed for me. You have taught me. You have blessed me. Thank you!

Look what the Lord has done!

Foreword

You believe the truth that God loves you and does not reject you. You've asked God to help you see your life from His perspective. But people have rejected you, they've disappointed you, they've lied to you and they've hurt you. How can you possibly forgive them and receive God's promise of healing? Can you risk trusting Him? Today you're full of faith and belief, tomorrow you're not so sure. You need help to walk in truth and healing on a day to day basis. Healing is sometimes instantaneous, but sometimes it's a process of allowing your mind & heart to be retrained by God's word.

This devotional by Angie Wynn will help you set your mind on God's truth every day.

Love Notes for the Rejected began in Angie's heart as she worked through her own healing. Rejection has many manifestations & the love notes she shares in this book were born out of the personal discipline required as she walked out her journey to freedom from rejection. It has been a privilege to walk alongside her as she has trusted God to continue her healing.

We love you Angie. We believe in you and we look forward to watching what God will do with the powerful voice He's put within you. Thank you for this tool that God can use to bless His people who desire to work through their own healing from rejection.

Dan and Jill Spiegelberg
Elijah House Facilitators
The Rock Family Worship Center, Huntsville, AL

Love Notes for the Rejected will uplift, encourage, and empower a broken spirit. One of the last tricks of the enemy is to cause such deep rooted wounds of rejection, abandonment, fear, loneliness, lack of self-worth, and many other issues. In this sweet, precious book, one can find peace, love, mercy, grace, and healing. Angie Wynn is a godly woman who has a heart for the lost, loveless, and broken-hearted women and men everywhere. Angie has experienced these same issues herself, so this precious book comes not only from her heart, but also from the heart of God. He wants to see His children healed and living whole, not depending on anyone, any substance, or anything else but Him. These Spirit-filled daily devotions accomplish just that! You will feel the presence of God and His love wrap around you and bring healing through His Holy Spirit. I highly recommend this book to everyone who has suffered from these ploys of the enemy. Thank you, Angie, for hearing straight from the throne room and creating such a healing daily devotional. This is one book I will use over and over with my clients and myself.

Rev. Robin Taylor
Pastoral Counselor
Bridge Crosser Ministries
Rainbow City, AL.

Introduction

In the following pages, you will find words that reflect the heart of God towards you. They are written in the form of "Love Notes" and addressed to you - His Beloved. As you read, *Love Notes for the Rejected*, I hope you will be enlightened, encouraged and energized by the love the Father has for you!

After each Love Note, you will encounter "Our Song." These song selections are intended to set the atmosphere of your heart as you prepare to write a "Love Note" back to the Lover of Your Soul in the spaces provided after each "Love Note " from Him. You can also choose your own "love song" for each Love Note. You can find all of the suggested songs in this book on the internet, for free, on sites such as You Tube, Yahoo Music, Vevo, and more.

I am excited for you to begin this journey of understanding your value in the heart of your Creator. It does not matter how long you have felt rejected, why you've felt rejected, or who rejected you. When you truly comprehend you are accepted and loved by the One True and Living God, it's all good!

May you be healed, delivered, and set free from all the wounds of rejection!

P.S.

Remember to join my mailing and be one of the first 500 readers to get your FREE download of *"Out of Darkness"* by Cindy Grate.

x

Love Notes

Endorsements iii

Acknowledgments v

Foreword vii

Introduction ix

Your Creator 13

The One Who Sees You 17

The One Who Rebuilds and Restores 21

Your Gift Giver 25

Your Life Giver 29

The Approver 33

Your Bondage Breaker 37

The Lover of Your Soul 41

The One Who Fights for You 45

Your Living Water 49

Your Thirst Quencher 53

The Keeper of Time 57

The Light of Your Life 61

Abba 65

The One Who Gives Beauty for Ashes 69

I AM Your Truth 73

I AM Your One True God 77

Your Perfect Love 81

The One Who Speaks Life 85

Your Sweet Aroma 89

Your Strong Tower 93

Your Grace Giver 97

Your Light 101

I AM Greater 105

I AM With You 109

I AM Life 113

The One Who Knows Rejection 117

I AM Your Peace 121

I AM Light and Life 125

Your Savior 129

About the Author 135

Contact Angie 137

Day 1

Your Creator

For You created my inmost being; You knit me together in my mother's womb. I praise You because I am fearfully and wonderfully made; Your works are wonderful, I know that full well.
Psalm 139:13

Love Notes for the Rejected

My Beloved,

    I knew you before the world began. More than that, I loved you before you were conceived, planned, or even imagined. There was never a time when I did not love you. You have never been invisible to Me. I imagined everything about you before I created you. Your eyes sparkle with light that comes from My Presence. I chose the color of your eyes. Your smile is a replica of My Smile as I formed you and took delight in you. The texture and color of your hair compliment your face. Your physical beauty is My Creation. Every skin cell, blood cell, bone, and muscle was designed for your good and My Pleasure. I am pleased with My Artistic Perfection in you. There is no one exactly like you. You are unique. Your design is intricate. You are My Masterpiece.

Your Creator

Our Song~ "Glorious" (Martha Munizzi)

As you encounter each reflection of you; may you be reminded of how much you are loved.

To My Creator,

Day 2

The One Who Sees You

My frame was not hidden from You when I was made in the secret place, when I was woven together in the depths of the earth. Your eyes saw my unformed body; all the days ordained for me were written in Your book before one of them came to be.

Psalm 139:15-16

My Beloved,

    I AM always conscious of your existence. I would not be who I say I AM if I did not acknowledge you. You will never be a victim of mistaken identity with Me. I recognize you. You are not a stranger. I know your name. You are a part of Me. You are always on My Mind and in My Heart. I recognized you in your mother's womb. I will recognize you when you are old and gray. Your existence is sound. Your life is valid because I created you. I love your authenticity. You are My Genuine Gift to humanity. The world would not be complete without you.

The One Who Sees You

Our Song ~ "I Am Not Forgotten"
(Israel Houghton)

 May you grow in knowledge and understanding of how well you are known, accepted, and valued.

To The One Who Sees Me,

Day 3

The One Who Rebuilds and Restores

Remember, Lord Your Great Mercy and Love, for they are from old. Do not remember the sins of my youth and my rebellious ways; according to Your Love remember me, for You Lord, are Good.
Psalm 25:6-7

My Beloved,

    I do not *tolerate* you. I accept you. I know that your life is a journey. I AM concerned but not surprised by detours. All has been filtered through My Hands of love. You have never made a choice that could not be covered by My Mercy. There are no physical, emotional, mental, or circumstantial changes that could ever affect My Love for you. I AM eager during those times to teach you more about Me and My Love for you. My Plans for you remain. I do not take back My Gifts and Callings. Your life is a love story between you and Me. Each chapter is woven with the good and bad, the ups and downs, victories and challenges that culminate in the beauty of your life that I designed for your good and My Pleasure.

The One Who Rebuilds and Restores

Our Song ~ "Great Is Your Mercy"
(Donnie McClurken)

 May Goodness and Mercy follow you all the days of your life.

24 | Love Notes for the Rejected

To The One Who Rebuilds and Restores,

DAY 4

Your Gift Giver

For God's Gifts and His Callings are irrevocable.
Romans 11:29

Love Notes for the Rejected

My Beloved,

    Why are you hiding? Why do you try to conceal what I have affirmed as special? I selected, designed, and designated your extraordinary gifts and talents. I have given them to you for a purpose. No one can do what you do as you do. If offering your gifts makes you fearful, I have a suggestion. If your gift is to sing, sing to Me. If your gift is to dance, dance for Me. If your gift is to speak, speak to Me. I will delight in you! You do not have to perform Just be who I created you to be. There is no risk of judgment or criticism with Me. And, as you share your gifts with Me, I will even calm your fears. In your freedom, the power of your gifts will accomplish My Plan for your life in this world, then you and I will be satisfied.

Your Gift Giver

Our Song ~ "Something About My Praise"
(Vicki Yohe)

May every opportunity to share your gift fill you with joy and contentment.

To My Gift Giver,

Day 5

Your Life Giver

The thief comes only to steal and kill and destroy; I have come that they may have life, and have it to the full.
John 10:10

Love Notes for the Rejected

My Beloved,

    I want you to embrace life. That is why I created you. I want you to experience the pleasure of witnessing both the sunrise and the sunset. I want you to marvel at the moon and the stars. I want you to enjoy the view from the heights of the mountains and the beauty that lies in the depths of the sea. I want you to laugh when you feel the warm sand between your toes and anticipate the delight of the cool ocean water that follows. I want you to smile when you feel My Caress in the breeze that plays beautiful music on the wind chimes which brings peace to your soul. I had you in mind when I fashioned this world and held nothing back. I did it for you.

Your Life Giver

Our Song~ "I Know My Redeemer Lives"
(Nicole C. Mullen)

As you encounter the beauty of the world around you, remember, I did it for you.

To My Life Giver,

Day 6

The Approver

Am I now trying to win the approval of human beings, or of God? Or am I trying to please people? If I were still trying to please people, I would not be a servant of Christ.
Galatians 1:10

My Beloved,

    My Heart breaks when I watch you work so hard to achieve the approval of others. In your own strength, you strive to talk the right way, dress the right way, and behave the right way. You do not limit this mindset or these actions to your earthly friends and family, but towards Me as well. Your performance may serve you well for a season. By some standards, you may even acquire success.

    The truth is, emotionally it has caused you much disappointment, sorrow, and loss. I watch you hurt and I AM grieved. And now, you grow weary in your efforts to "measure up."

    I desperately want you to know, in My Eyes, no one compares to you. I love your being, not your doing. Cease striving. Rest, and be reassured you have My Approval. After all, I AM the Only One that really matters.

The Approver

Love Notes for the Rejected | 35

Our Song ~ "I Will Rejoice" (Rita Springer)

 Where your feet trod you will possess the land; and everything you place your hand to will prosper as you trust in Me and not your own efforts and strength. Rejoice and be glad!

Love Notes for the Rejected

To My Approver,

Day 7

Your Bondage Breaker

He will wipe every tear from their eyes. There will be no more death or mourning or crying or pain; for the old order of things has passed away.
Revelation 21:4

Love Notes for the Rejected

My Beloved,

There have been times when we have not spoken. I perceived your anger towards Me. You had your expectations of Me in your life. You planned outcomes that did not happen. The people that should have loved you, did not. The people that should have protected you, did not. That position went to someone else. That relationship ended. Instead of being celebrated, you were ignored or forgotten. You felt justified in your disappointment with them and with Me. Your soul was wounded. You cried many tears. What you did not realize is that I had a reason and a strategy.

Those people, places, and things along with your expectations were hindrances. They summoned you to perform to be accepted. It was too hard and too much work for you! I could not stand by and watch that happen. I did for you what you were unable to do for yourself. I loved you enough to bring you out of captivity into the promised land of freedom.

Your Bondage Breaker

Our Song ~ "For Every Mountain" (Kurt Carr)

In and through every circumstance, may you walk in the freedom of faith; free from the bondage of expectations and outcomes.

To My Bondage Breaker,

Day 8

The Lover of Your Soul

For the Lord your God is Living among you. He is a Mighty Savior. He will take delight in you with gladness. With His Love, He will calm all your fears. He will rejoice over you with joyful songs.
Zephaniah 3:17

My Beloved,

    I long to help you understand that I desire to be with you. I AM pursuing a love relationship with you. Even now, you cannot go anywhere without Me. I AM orchestrating everything in your life to lead to a lasting, loving relationship with Me. From your conception, I knew that people would fail you, intentionally and unintentionally. I knew there would be voids in your life that would hurt you, and those open wounds in your soul would need My Attention and Healing. I wanted you to stay close. Many times when the ones you loved walked away or disappointed you, I wanted you to hear Me whisper "I love you." You are My child. There is a void for Me when you do not communicate. I need to understand your feelings. I need to hear your voice. I need to know you. I want you to always approach Me with that confidence.

The Lover of Your Soul

Our Song ~ "To Worship You I Live."
(Israel Houghton)

 As you saturate your soul in My Presence, through worship and the Word, may your healing be swift and complete.

To The Lover of My Soul,

Day 9

The One Who Fights for You

I sought the Lord, and He answered me; He delivered me from all my fears. Those who look to Him are radiant; their faces are never covered with shame. This poor man called, and the Lord heard him; He saved him out of all his troubles.

Psalm 34:4-6

Love Notes for the Rejected

My Beloved

 Shame has been a heavy burden that you have carried. Shame has been a living thing. Shame has been a vile thing. Shame is the name of the cancer that has sought to kill and destroy your soul. You embraced shame. But I say to you today – shame is not your name. It is not your identity. It has been placed upon you by yourself and others. The underlying root of shame is misunderstanding, lack of love, and fear, cloaked in condemning words and actions. I Am the cure for shame. I Am the One who delivers you from shame. I remove the tumor, the growth, the disease. I Am calling you forth to live in beauty and boldness with confidence and courage that defeats shame and puts it to death. Let Me be the One who lifts your head. Look to Me. I Am the One who is Faithful. I Am the One who moves mountains. Let Me be your Strong Tower. I Am the Heavyweight Champion of your soul for which there are no other competent contenders!

The One Who Fights for You

Our Song ~ "I Have to Believe" (Rita Springer)

This day you have been delivered from shame; from the top of your head to the soles of your feet, you are forgiven...you are healed...you are free!

Love Notes for the Rejected

To The One Who Fights for Me,

Day 10

Your Living Water

Bear with each other and forgive one another if any of you has a grievance against someone. Forgive as the Lord forgave you.
Colossians 3:13

Love Notes for the Rejected

My Beloved,

    Inhale Deeply. Just Breathe. Quietly. There are times when the painful memories of the ones who hurt you and rejected you surface. I would like to tell you two things you may not know about them. First, they were experiencing their own hurt and rejection; and second, they had no idea the depth of pain they were inflicting on you. I can assure you that I have brought to their remembrance the circumstances between you and them. In love, I Am working in their hearts for them to own their part, forgive themselves, and be willing to express love and forgiveness toward you. You must receive this Truth. I created all of you. I see all of you. I know all of you. I am working all things out for the good of each of you. I Am drawing each of you to Myself for a refreshing drink of Living Water that heals and restores. Now....drink of this cup of forgiveness and love.

Your Living Water

Our Song ~ "The Sea of Forgetfulness"
    (Helen Baylor)

 May you be empowered to forgive as I have forgiven you.

52 | Love Notes for the Rejected

To My Living Water,

DAY 11

Your Thirst Quencher

In their hunger You gave them bread from heaven and in their thirst You brought them water from the rock.
Nehemiah 9:15

My Beloved

    Your heart is alive. Your heart can be hungry. Your heart can be thirsty. Nutrition is vital for a healthy heart. Every message your mind receives about Me, yourself and others begins in your heart. Living things have two basic needs: nourishment to survive and thrive and protection from disease and death. The world and the flesh serve meals of un-forgiveness, fear, anger, rejection, pain, and strife. You have failed to thrive on that menu. It does nothing to quench your thirst. The taste is bitter and it is bad for your heart. I Am the Master Chef. My delicacies are pure and heart healthy. The meat of My Word will strengthen your heart. My Will is the Bread of Life that you will desire. The sweet fruit of My Ways will continue to create in you an enthusiastic appetite for My Presence. Feast at My table, and you will be satisfied. Drink of My Living Water, and you will be filled.

Your Thirst Quencher

Love Notes for the Rejected | **55**

Our Song ~ "We Thirst for You"
(Cee Cee Winans)

 Take and drink of My Love; you will never thirst again.

To My Thirst Quencher,

DAY 12

The Keeper of Time

There is a time for everything, and a season for every activity under the heavens.
Ecclesiastes 3:1

My Beloved,

There is no concern or conflict in Me regarding time. Settle that matter in your heart. I Am the Alpha and Omega — The Beginning and The End. I existed before time began as you understand it. I AM already in Eternity. Be certain all of your circumstances are at the right time, with no need to worry about time spent or wasted. There is no such thing. If you allow Me, I can use time to your advantage. In time - you learn. In time - you grow. In time - you understand. In time - you forgive. In time, you heal. In time, things change. All you need to understand about time is this; now is the time for you to receive the love and acceptance I have for you. There is no lack in Me. I have loved you with an Everlasting Love. It is full and it is free. Rest in it and be satisfied. It is time.

The Keeper of Time

Our Song ~ "I'll Always Remember"
(Damaris Carbaugh)

 May you walk in freedom regarding time; having faith that in the fullness of time, all will be well for you in Me.

To The Keeper of Time,

Day 13

The Light of Your Life

You, Lord, are my lamp; the Lord turns my darkness into light. With your help I can advance against a troop; with my God I can scale a wall.
2 Samuel 22:29-30

Love Notes for the Rejected

My Beloved,

    You have probably heard the saying, "Come out of the shadows." That statement reflects My desire for you. I want you to be free from the shadow of rejection. A shadow is an area of darkness resulting from an obstruction of light. It is solitary. It is gloomy. It is empty. It has no power, purpose, or plan. It is distorted. It is unrelenting. It follows you wherever you go. Hear Me – shadows are primarily found on a wall or on the ground. I never wanted that for you. I created you for so much more. A huge price was paid so you would not have to live in darkness. You have substance, essence, texture, and light. You are a radiant reflection of Me. It brings Me pleasure for My Glorious Light to be seen in you.

The Light of Your Life

Love Notes for the Rejected | 63

Our Song ~ "You Amaze Me" (Vicki Yohe)

"Arise, shine for your light has come, and the Glory of the Lord rises upon you." (Isaiah 60:1)

To The Light of My Life,

Day 14

Abba

God sets the lonely in families.
Psalm 68:6

My Beloved,

    I AM the Author of Surrogacy. Before you were conceived, the pain of the rejection you would experience in your life was of utmost concern to Me. I knew you would need and desire a relationship, which to you, seemed missing. I knew you would need and desire a family that seemed absent. But I had a plan to fill in the missing pieces and create presence out of absence. I long to fill your empty places with life more abundant.

    I know you did not understand completely, but I sent many people to love you. There were men and women who spoke words of affirmation and kindness and life to you. Those that loved you and nurtured you and taught you were sent from Me. Even the ones that corrected you were sent to help you and guide you on the path of life I designed.

    The owner of the corner store was like an uncle who would let you have an extra treat free of charge. That doctor who took extra time with you was like the Grandfather you never met. Your classmates were like your brothers and sisters. The church members you spent Thanksgiving with were all sent from Me. I will bring them to your remembrance and I will reveal their purpose. Then, you will understand it was never My plan to leave you lost and lonely. I fathered you.

Abba

    Our Song ~ "The Father's Love Letter"
              (Barry Adams)

 Today, you are no longer an orphan. Receive My love.

To Abba,

DAY 15

The One Who Gives Beauty for Ashes

There is no fear in love; but perfect love casts out fear: because fear has torment. He that fears is not made perfect in love.

I John 4:18

My Beloved,

    I have witnessed the many, many times you have cried because you have felt rejected. Wherever the injury came from, whether it was the circumstances, the relationship, the conflict, or the misunderstanding, your self-inflicted wounds were more life threatening than any other issue. Your burning questions were always the same. What did I do to make them treat me this way? Why don't they love me like I need to be loved? Why did they go away? The burden you carried was always too great. Your wounded soul bore all the responsibility. You responded - to them and to yourself by building walls and becoming angry; but most of all, you became fearful. You became consumed by the fear of not ever being loved. It has been your torment. You have punished yourself again and again. Your punishment has only produced more pain.

    I challenge you now: as I give you the strength and the courage to exchange your hurt for My healing, your punishment and pain for My perfection. No other love can satisfy you like Mine. No other love can soothe you like

Mine. No other love can save you like Mine. I love you flawlessly.

The One Who Gives Beauty for Ashes

Our Song ~ "What Can Separate You?"
(Babbie Mason)

 Receive this word, nothing and no one can or will ever separate you from My perfect love.

Love Notes for the Rejected

To the One Who Gives Beauty for Ashes,

Day 16

I AM Your Truth

*Listen daughter, and pay careful attention: Forget your people and your father's house. Let the King be enthralled by your beauty; honor Him, for He is your Lord."
Psalm 45:10-11*

Love Notes for the Rejected

My Beloved,

You have believed some lies about Me that have affected our relationship. I AM ready to settle the dispute. This is Truth. Your conception was not a mistake. You were not born to the wrong people at the wrong time, even if that's what they told you. You are in the right skin. You are the right gender. You are in the right place at this moment. You are wonderfully made. You are lovable. I created you, and I AM delighted in you! I AM peace. I AM not drama. I do not lie.

Do not design a role for yourself as a victim of people or circumstances. Do not allow the actions and voices of people to hinder your understanding of Me - whether family, friends, or loved ones.

I AM the Alpha and the Omega, the Beginning and the End. My love for you did not begin with the and it will not end with them. My love also covers you in the middle. Their opinion and, yes, even yours is of no effect. Opinion is not necessarily Truth. Truth is Truth. Believe it. Receive it.

I AM Your Truth

Our Song ~ "I Believe God" (Martha Munizzi)

You are released from every lie that has hindered you.

Love Notes for the Rejected

To My Truth,

Day 17

I AM Your One True God

Who shapes a god and casts an idol which can profit him nothing.
Isaiah 44:10

Love Notes for the Rejected

My Beloved,

When you are unsure of My love for you, you wander. As you wander, you create idols along the way. Some of your idols are "things", material possessions. But most of your idols are people. Yes, some people are sent from Me, but some are of your own choosing. You look to your idols to make you feel better, to affirm you, to rescue you. You think for a moment their ways, their words, their love is just as good as or better than Mine. If, in your heart, you make a person an idol, consider this: most idols begin as soft, pliable, flexible materials but their final appearance is cold stone, unable to feel, nurture or love.

No human being, no matter how hard they try, can come close to the all-inclusive love I have for you. I love every fiber of your being. I love every breath you take and every beat of your heart. I know every thought, every fear, and every dream. I AM concerned about you and active and alive in every second that you live. Away with your hard, breathless, insensitive graven images and golden calves. I AM vibrant, I AM alert, I AM energetic, I AM quick, I AM full of life and I AM yours.

I AM Your One True God

Our Song ~ "You Alone Are God" (Marvin Sapp)

Today, and in the days to come may every idol be revealed and cast down; and may you find every need met in My Presence, the One True, and Living God.

To My One True God,

DAY 18

Your Perfect Love

There is no fear in love. But perfect love casts out fear, because fear involves punishment, and the one who fears is not perfected in love.
1John 4:18

My Beloved,

As a child, you developed a definition of love born out of rejection and the need for your heart to survive. The ones that you wanted to love you, whether real or perceived, were always away from you, so you formed this equation in your heart: love + longing = love. This has been the foundation of your walls of protection to prevent your pain and suffering and rejection. It has also been the walls of your prison. Many times, you have locked yourself away from loving up close. You have been more comfortable loving from a distance. This has served you well for a season.

As you live, learn, and grow, your desires are changing. You need more. You want more. You want to close. I AM More. I AM Close. Steal away with Me, come close to Me, and I will redefine your definition of love. I will retrain and reprogram your heart. The truth is this: love + longing = fear. Being fearful is tormenting. Fear and love cannot coexist in your heart.

Let Me protect you as you learn to truly love. Your heart is safe with Me.

Your Perfect Love

Our Song ~ "I Could Sing of Your Love Forever"
(Hillsong)

 As I give you the courage to draw near to Me, doubts and fears will be put to death. Assurance will come that I will never leave you or forsake you.

To My Perfect Love,

Day 19

The One Who Speaks Life

You shall not bow down to them or worship them; for I, the Lord your God am a jealous God.
Exodus 20:5

Do not worship any other god, for the Lord, whose name is Jealous, is a jealous God.
Exodus 34:14

My Beloved,

    If you listen very attentively, you can hear My Voice. There are so many things I want to say to you. I have been jealous that you have taken to heart the voices that have burdened, belittled, rejected, and condemned you. My sheep hear My Voice. They will not follow a stranger's voice. Do not listen to those words that bring death to dreams, visions, hope, or confidence in Me. My Voice speaks life. My Presence brings joy. If you turn your ear to Me, this is what you will hear: I AM here. I love you. I AM pleased with you. I know you. I forgive you. Come closer. Let me show you. I AM the One who will work it all out for your good and My Glory.

The One Who Speaks Life

Love Notes for the Rejected

Our Song ~ "God is Here" (Martha Munizzi)

May you hear My voice continuously speak of My never-ending love towards you.

To The One Who Speaks Life,

Day 20

Your Sweet Aroma

But thanks be to God, who always leads us in triumphal procession in Christ and through us spreads everywhere the fragrance of the knowledge of Him.
2Corinthians 2:14

My Beloved,

Religion has taught you that the Christian Life is only about Me and other people. Codependency has taught you that it is wrong to take care of you. These mindsets have promoted the lie that your life does not have worth or value – that you are insignificant. It is true, the two Greatest Commandments are to love Me with your whole heart, and your neighbor as yourself. However, instead of asking you to "work" to love your neighbor and Me, I want to teach you to "walk" in love as you are loved.

Think of love as a pleasant perfume. It flows from you into the atmosphere and those who encounter you enjoy the fragrance. In fact, it brings such pleasure, that they often look for the source of that sweet aroma as well as ask the name. There are different measures of applying fragrance: you can splash, spray, or saturate.

The decision begins with you, and others experience it in that portion. And so it is with love. Soaking in My love for you validates your being, not your doing. I experience your love as you look for Me. As others encounter you, they will be drawn. They will ask for the source, and you will tell them My Name. My Name brings relationship not religion or rejection. In My Name and with My Love is how you keep the Greatest Commandments. This is what brings Me pleasure.

Your Sweet Aroma

Our Song ~ "Say the Name" (Martha Munizzi)

May your existence be like sweet incense to everyone you encounter.

92 | Love Notes for the Rejected

To My Sweet Aroma,

DAY 21

Your Strong Tower

No one is like You Lord; You are Great, and Your Name is Mighty in Power.
Jeremiah 10:6

My Beloved,

    You are gifted. You are called. You have an assignment. You have purpose. You also possess power. Because of Me, you walk into a room and change the atmosphere. Eyes marvel. Heads turn. Chains fall. There is no competition, but there is an enemy. He wants to silence your voice by simply reminding you of your struggles. Silly enemy. You already know them, and so do I. My Grace is able to keep you. More than that, before the foundation of the world, I chose you to arrive at the place of your assignment, to the people of your assignment, with the promise of victory.

    You are powerful to set the captives free...in My Name. You are poised to plant the seeds of life and blessing because of the pain that you have pushed through....in My Name. Walk with me. Let's enjoy this journey. Rejection has no place here.

Your Strong Tower

Our Song ~ "Till the Walls Fall"
 (Martha Munizzi)

You will never fail or fall as you trust in the power of My Name.

To My Strong Tower,

Day 22

Your Grace Giver

Now I commit you to God and to the Word of His Grace, which can build you up and give you an inheritance among all those who are sanctified.

Acts 20:32

My Beloved,

    There is something I AM desperate for you to change. I have been a Witness to your words. There has been much self-condemnation, self-criticism, and self-pity out of your mouth. You have based your worth on what you and others have thought about you and your experiences without considering Me and what I have done for you. Do you remember reading in My Word that everything I created was good? If I were not your Creator, your words would make you unrecognizable to Me. My Great Grace and My Mercy have found you and have given you a voice. Your miracle is in your mouth. Your words have power. I want you to speak life over yourself! Agree with Me. "I am accepted. My Father God loves me. He values me. Because of His Grace I have tremendous worth in His sight. I am not rejected."

Your Grace Giver

Our Song ~ "Your Grace Finds Me"
(Matt Redman)

 As you walk and talk and live, breathe My Grace.

100 | Love Notes for the Rejected

To My Grace Giver,

Day 23

Your Light

See, darkness is over the Earth and thick darkness is over the peoples; but the Lord rises upon you and His Glory appears over you.
Isaiah 60:2

My Beloved,

When you encounter the ones who hurt you, give Me room to move. Let Me explain. You are so used to the pain of rejection that you set your position and your posture to defend your right to "be" - to be present in their midst, to be acknowledged in their midst, to be treated with respect, to be heard. The sacrifice of My Son was so you could live in confident authenticity, not constant antagonism. Your heart always betrays itself in your face. This invites the opposition. Never let them see you fret. Instead, grasp this Truth. I have given you the right to be. Light always conquers darkness. In your body, My light looks like this: your head lifted and your back straight with a smile on your face. In your soul, My Light is My voice speaking to you, "I am His Beloved." The Light of My Spirit that lives within you shines confidently and brightly even on your enemies.

Your Light

Our Song ~ "Oh Fear (My God is Near)"
(Moriah Peters)

Walk confidently in the Light that lives in you.

Love Notes for the Rejected

To My Light,

DAY 24

I AM Greater

You, dear children, are from God and have overcome them, because the One who is in you is Greater than the one who is in the world.
1 John 4:4

My Beloved,

When you accept My love for you, some exchanges will be a part of your journey: truth for lies, faith for fear, resting for striving, freedom for bondage, healing for sickness, birthing for barrenness, destiny for doubting, courage for timidity, obedience for rebellion, honor for shame, and abundance for emptiness. You will exchange your "natural" life for a "supernatural" life; which simply means that many times the exchange will defy logic or reason. Things will work out for your good just because of your relationship with Me. There is nothing that can be compared to a life in Me. You have lived too long in lack! You have been desperate for horizontal relationships to fill you. But no person will ever satisfy you completely. There is no one more capable of helping you than Me. There is no one more willing to help you than Me. There is nothing and no one greater in your life than Me.

I AM Greater

Our Song ~ "Nobody Greater"
(VaShawn Mitchell)

 I AM The One who is Great and I have a wonderful plan for your life.

108 | Love Notes for the Rejected

To I AM Greater,

Day 25

I AM With You

He has caused His wonders to be remembered.
Psalm 111:4

My Beloved,

    I have a history with you. Every long-term relationship has a history. I want you always to remember how we met. I want you to remember when you first heard My Voice and My first Words. Do you remember when you first experienced My Presence? I was with you in the Sanctuary when the weight of My Glory was felt. I have never left you. Remember the night I rescued you in the middle of the madness? You were so afraid. I rose to help you when I witnessed that injustice and abuse. I never want you to experience that again. Our alone times are the ones I have treasured the most. There are no lies, no pretense, no fear. You are safe. You are known. Rejection is never an issue.

I AM With You

Our Song ~ Who Is Like the Lord?
(Israel Houghton)

When the heaviness of rejection tries to weigh you down, remember My kindness and love as I drew you to Myself and still draw you even closer.

To I AM With You,

Day 26

I AM Life

He was despised and rejected by men, a Man of Sorrows, and familiar with suffering...
Isaiah 53:3

My Beloved,

    When you are in the throes of feeling rejected, you "wear" rejection like a shroud. It distorts everything you see and experience and every relationship. In those times, you are capable of making some poor decisions. You give of yourself too much, in hopes of an exchange for love. You forget My standards in love relationships in order to simply experience human touch. You had seasons when you lost your identity to gain man's approval, affection, and acceptance. You have been willing to lose your life so others would help you live. I acknowledge your desperation, and My heart longs to set you free!

    Allow Me to commute your self-inflicted death sentence. You don't have to die for people, for I already made the death sacrifice in the person of My Son Jesus. He was despised and rejected, so you did not have to be. His Death and Resurrection entitles you to "all things" – love and acceptance and freedom. Look to Him and live.

I AM Life

Our Song ~ "Renew Me" (Martha Munizzi)

Rejection has been credited and paid for. Your heart has been ransomed. You are released. It is finished.

Love Notes for the Rejected

To I AM Life,

Day 27

The One Who Knows Rejection

The Lord your God, who is going before you, will fight for you, as He did for you in Egypt, before your very eyes.
Deuteronomy 1:30

Love Notes for the Rejected

My Beloved,

    I AM very familiar with rejection. It has been a part of My existence even before man was created. It started with rebellion among the angels. An angel close to Me who was beautifully adorned and trusted with worship was the leader of that uprising. Jealousy, envy, strife, and rejection were all birthed in Heaven against Me. When I created mankind, the plot continued. I AM the God of the Universe and I walked with them in that Garden because I loved them. They rejected My Presence, My Position, and My Plan and believed lies about Me instead. The same is true for My Son and for My Spirit.

    When rejection comes, I cannot fold. I cannot hide. I cannot retreat. I AM. I created you in My image, so you also are able to choose not to hide, fold, or retreat. This is the truth - when others reject you, it does not diminish your identity. There is no loss of power unless you give it away. You can still love. You can still hope. You can still stand in the presence of the ones who reject you. I AM.

The One Who Knows Rejection

Our Song ~ "Amazing God" (William Murphy)

I will hold you in My right hand, and remind you that you can love, hope, and stand in the face of rejection.

To The One Who Knows Rejection,

Day 28

I AM Your Peace

In your anger, do not sin.
Ephesians 4:26

Love Notes for the Rejected

My Beloved,

    I have witnessed the times when your rejection spilled over in the form of anger. Once, or twice it was an explosion of epic proportions. Every ounce of pain was released at that moment on the person that perhaps unknowingly reopened the wound of rejection. You, the victim attacked.

    More often, your anger can be an insidious mixture of self-pity, pride, and impatience. Your hidden thoughts are full of manipulation and the need to control. If the ones who attacked in anger, let you have your way, did what you wanted them to do, when you wanted them to do it, that would have felt like love and answered all your need for love and acceptance. If they did not comply with your control, your sweetness became sullen. Their punishment became your silence or your sarcasm. Your cure became your own poison.

    I understand why you get angry and I have great compassion for you. However, I AM grieved when you behave that way. It affects you negatively - body, soul, and spirit. When you feel so rejected, whether the rejection is real or perceived and the anger rises, talk to Me. I will listen. I will affirm you. I will comfort you. I will diffuse your disappointment before it detonates. Come with expectation. My Cure will be your peace.

I AM Your Peace

>Our Song ~ Waiting Here for You
> (Christy Nockels)

 May your soul be far from anxiety and fear and anger. I will keep you in perfect peace.

Love Notes for the Rejected

To My Peace,

DAY 29

I AM Light and Life

God blessed them and said to them, "Be fruitful and multiply and increase in number...
Genesis 1:28

In the same way, let your light shine before others, that they may see your good deeds and glorify your Father in Heaven.
Matthew 5:16

Love Notes for the Rejected

My Beloved,

There is one sure way to know that you are truly living. Living things have a purpose. Living things grow, reproduce, and multiply. I have given you gifts of the Spirit in order to accomplish your purpose. It is My heart for your very existence. It is confirmation that My Spirit is alive in you. I designed this so that you would not always focus on yourself which is a limited focus. My Message is limitless. It has no boundaries. I need you to carry the seed that will birth this Treasure in others. I need your presence, your voice, and your hands as the extensions of Mine.

A life of rejection is such a weak contrast to the powerful plan I have for you! So, let your presence in this life be a source of light and life. Allow your voice to be used as a trumpet to wake others who are in the daze and slumber of rejection. Agree that your hands will always be tools of comfort and safety to those who are hurting.

Reproduce the gift that you have been given. That brings Me good pleasure.

I AM Light and Life

>Our Song ~ Go Light Your World
>(Kathy Troccoli)

 May My light that shines in you never go dim.

Love Notes for the Rejected

To I AM Light and Life,

DAY 30

Your Savior

My sheep hear My voice: I know them, and they follow Me.
John 10:27

My Beloved,

    I speak and something happens. My Words bring life. Hearts are healed. Lives change. Let Me speak to your soul. You are important. You matter. You have value. You have worth. You are not rejected. You are loved.

    I Name and the Truth of your identity is revealed. Hear Me call you by name. I call you wanted. I call you special. I call you chosen. I call you My Beloved. I call you My Child. I call you My Friend.

    I bless and you begin to experience life more abundantly. Receive this Blessing. I AM the Only One True and Living God. I will never leave you or forsake you. You are not alone. You are not defeated. You are not rejected. Call upon Me when your heart needs to be rescued. I will rise to answer you.

Your Savior

Our Song ~ "Lord of All" (Kelly Price)

Receive My love and acceptance today.

To My Savior,

About the Author

When you meet Angie Wynn, it's hard to believe what her journey has been. She has survived many issues, including rejection, abandonment, and emotional, mental, and physical abuse. She gives the credit for her survival solely to her Lord and Savior Jesus Christ. Over the years, they have had many "Superman/Lois Lane" moments. He has been her Hero, who knows her completely and loves her unconditionally

Her academic achievements include a B.S. in Physical Therapy from Howard University, a Master's Degree in Christian Counseling from Life Management Institute, and inclusion in *Who's Who Among American Business Women 2007.* As a recipient of Christian Counseling, Angie became aware of the value of speaking life and healing and blessing into the lives of people who are hurting. She established "Transitions" Christian Counseling Service in 2007 and has been blessed to share the gift that she has been given through one-on -one counseling, speaking, teaching, and conferences. Her heart is to help others walk in the freedom of the abundant life God has promised.

Angie is a member of Silverdale Baptist Church where she has served as a Women's Ministry Teacher and Speaker.

Contact Angie

Angie Wynn is available for speaking at women's conferences, retreats, workshops, or other events. To request Angie for your next event please go to www.angiewynn.com and fill out a request.

Remember to join Angie's mailing and be one of the first 500 readers to get your FREE download of *"Out of Darkness"* by Cindy Grate.

www.ingramcontent.com/pod-product-compliance
Lightning Source LLC
Chambersburg PA
CBHW041627220426
43663CB00004B/90